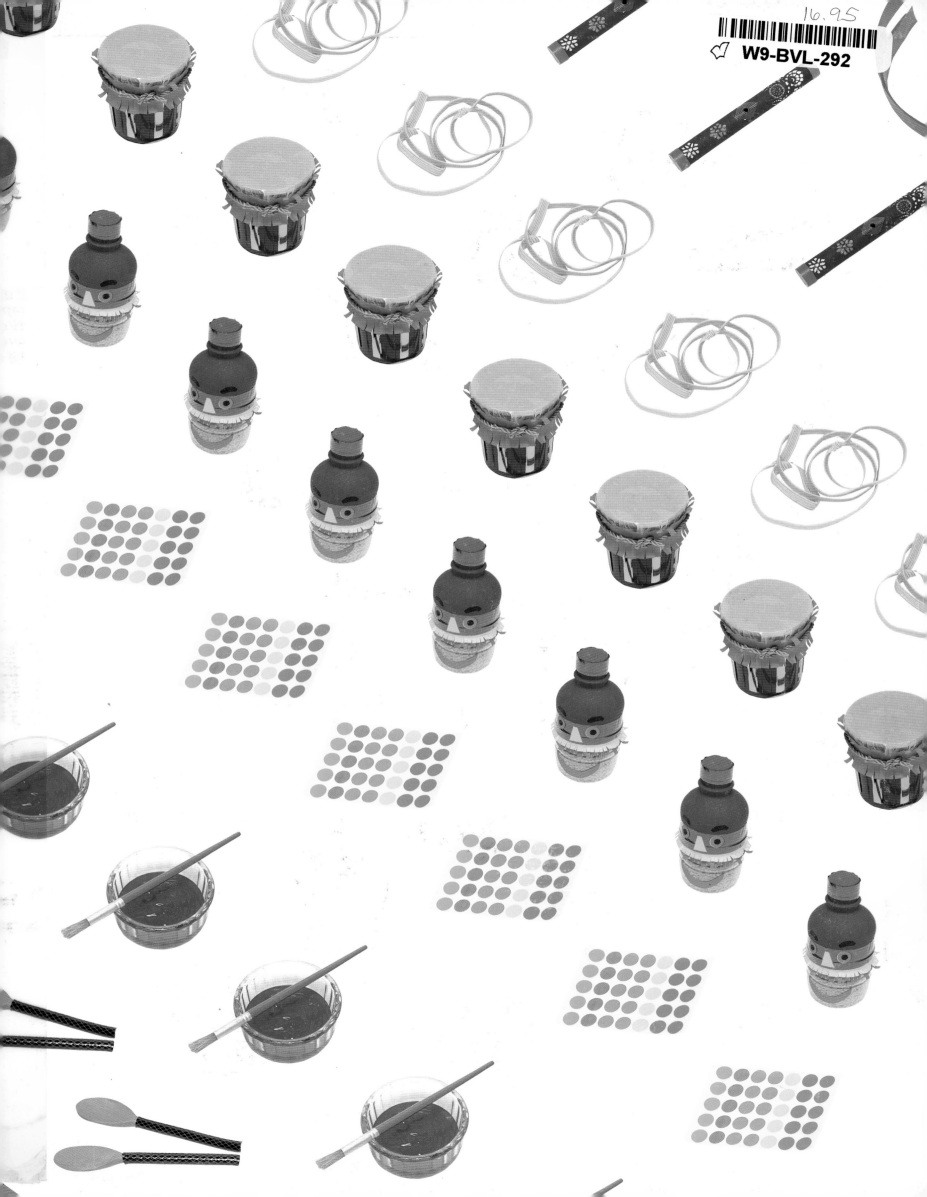

SHOW-ME-HOW
Can Make Music

Simple-to-make and fun-to-play
musical instruments for young children

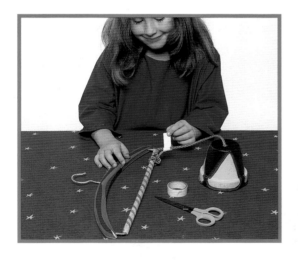

MICHAEL PURTON

SMITHMARK

This edition first published in 1996 by
SMITHMARK Publishers
a division of
U.S. Media Holdings, Inc.
16 East 32nd Street
New York, NY 10016

SMITHMARK books are available for bulk purchase for
sales promotion and premium use. For details write or call
the manager of special sales, SMITHMARK Publishers,
16 East 32nd Street, New York, NY 10016; (212) 532-6600.

ISBN 0-8317-7264-6

Publisher: Joanna Lorenz
Project Editor: Judith Simons
Text Editor: Judy Walker
Designer: Edward Kinsey
Photographer: John Freeman
Stylist: Thomasina Smith

Printed in China

PLEASE NOTE
The level of adult supervision needed will
depend on the age and ability of the children
following the projects. However,
we advise that adult supervision is always
preferable and vital if the project calls for the
use of sharp knives or other objects.
See the ▮ symbol for more information on
where adult help is needed.

ACKNOWLEDGEMENTS
The publishers would like to thank the
following children who were such wonderful
models, and their parents: Benjamin Ferguson,
Lorenzo Green, Nicholas Lie, Gabriella and
Izabella Malewska, Ilaira and Joshua Mallalieu,
Jessica and Alice Moxley, Alice Purton and
Claudius Wilson.

Contents

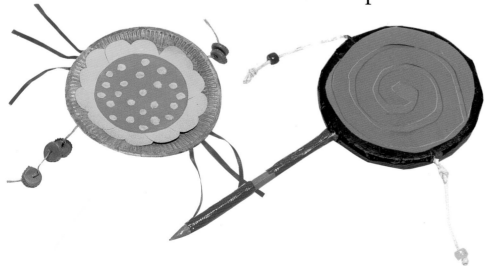

Introduction

What is music? Very simply, music is made from sounds that are pleasing or interesting to hear. Bird songs can be described as music and so can the sounds of the wind or the sea. Many people who write music – composers – have copied the sounds of nature in their music.

Sound is caused by vibrations in the air. The stronger the vibrations, the louder the sound. Musical instruments help us to make music by producing many different sounds. Your own voice is a musical instrument. See how many sounds you can make by altering the shape of your mouth, by using your tongue in different ways, and by changing the pitch of your voice from high to low. We are in fact a mixture of the different types of instruments described below: we are wind instruments because we use air to make sounds; stringed instruments because we speak or sing through our vocal cords, which are like strings low down in our throats; and percussion instruments because we can clap our hands and snap our fingers.

Musicians divide musical instruments into different groups:

Percussion Instruments

These are all the instruments that you hit. They were probably the earliest instruments. People from long ago made music by hitting bones together or hitting a hollow tree. Animal skins were stretched over pots or bits of tree trunks to make drums. It is not

Claudius has made a bugle which is a wind instrument.

Gabriella's bottle xylophone is a percussion instrument.

just drums that are percussion instruments. There are all kinds of fun shakers and rattles which are also used to give rhythm to music.

Wind Instruments

These are the instruments that you blow. The air vibrates inside the hollow instrument and makes a sound. The first instruments of this kind were made out of hollow animal horns or bones. Wind instruments sometimes have a "reed" to help make a good sound. A drinking straw works very well for this.

Stringed Instruments

These instruments can be plucked with your fingers or played with a bow. The strings were first made out of hair and silk. All stringed instruments need a hollow box of some kind over which the strings are attached. The box is full of air which vibrates when you play the instrument.

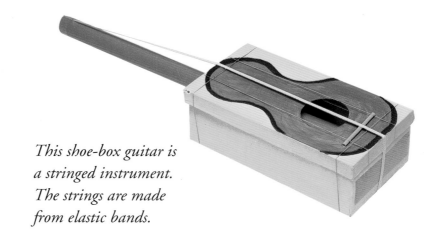

This shoe-box guitar is a stringed instrument. The strings are made from elastic bands.

Jessica is making a drum from a mini-plastic wastebasket.

Musical Families

See how many instruments you can think of, and try to place them in a family or group. Is the piano a stringed instrument? It has strings but they are not plucked or played with a bow. If you look inside the piano, you will see that small, felt hammers hit the strings to make the sounds. It is a percussion instrument!

Making Musical Instruments

This book will help you to discover lots of different sounds by making your own instruments and then playing them. They are very easy to make. All you need to make music is a cardboard tube or soda can and a few bottle caps or a shower cap! Some of the instruments come from countries like Africa and Latin America, so it is a good chance to decorate them with really bright colors. If you make one of the fun shakers or rattles, it will feel like carnival time!

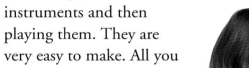

It's fun to make music with someone else to help.

Maracas are filled with rice or beans and make a wonderful sound when you shake them.

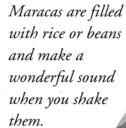

Making Music Together

It is even more fun playing music in groups. Perhaps you and your friends can each make a different instrument to play. First try a rhythm game. Each of you choose a word, and then play the rhythm (the beat) of that word on your instruments over and over again. Try to keep time with everyone else, then experiment by getting louder then softer, and slower then faster.

You could join in with your favorite pop song. Start with the percussion instruments to make the rhythm, then add a wind instrument like a kazoo to sing the tune. See how many different instruments you can use. Make up some music to describe a storm, a ghost story, or a trip to the zoo.

This reed pipe is a very simple kind of oboe made from a cardboard tube with a drinking straw for the "reed."

Equipment and Materials

All the musical instruments in this book are easy to make at home. There are some basic pieces of equipment and some craft materials that you will need to make and decorate the projects, such as paper, glue, paints, paintbrushes, scissors, and felt-tipped pens. If you look after your equipment and put all the pieces away when you have finished at the end of the day, they will last a long time, and you will be able to use them again and again.

Paper and cardboard. Brightly colored paper and cardboard are fun and quick to use. But you can use white cardboard and paper, instead, and decorate them in bright colors, using paints, colored stickers, or felt-tipped pens.

Stickers and string. You can get colored stickers in lots of shapes and sizes, and use them to brighten up your musical instruments. Colored string can be used to decorate your instruments, too.

Paints and paintbrushes. There are many different kinds of paint, but the easiest to use are acrylic paints or poster paints. You can mix them with water to make them thin and watery, or use them thick if you want a very bright color. If you are using more than one color, have several brushes to work with – one for each color. Rinse out your brushes with water as soon as you have finished, otherwise the paint will harden and stick to them.

Paint pots. These are pots with special lids which stop the paint from spilling if you knock them over by mistake. They are very useful if you want to mix up a lot of paint and save some to use later. Wash out the pots with clean water before you put a different color in them.

Felt-tipped pens. These are great to use for decorating. Some are water-based and wash off your hands and clothes easily. The colors cannot be mixed like paints, so it is best to use them separately.

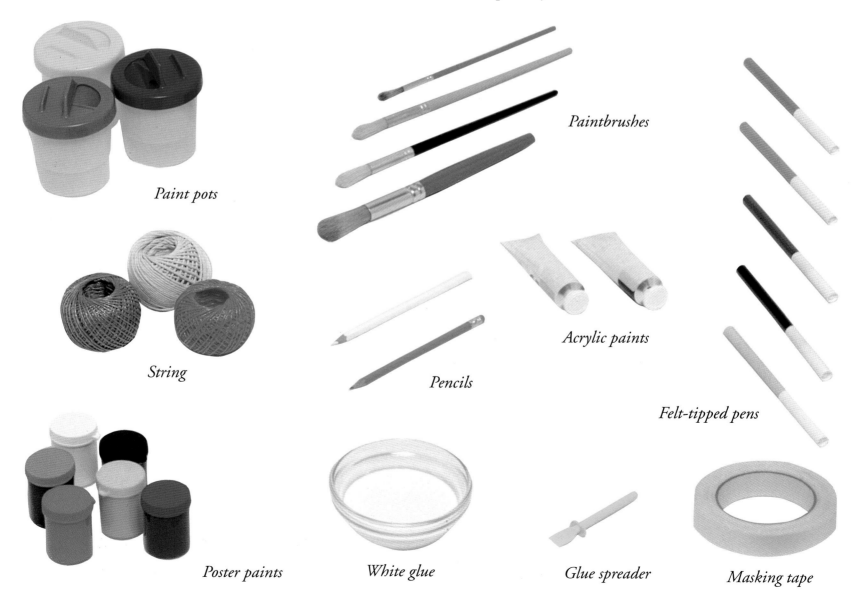

Paint pots

Paintbrushes

String

Acrylic paints

Pencils

Felt-tipped pens

Poster paints

White glue

Glue spreader

Masking tape

Glues. White glue is best to use because it washes off your hands and brushes. It is white to begin with, but when it dries, it becomes invisible. You can apply it with a glue brush or a glue spreader. It will stick most things together – wood, paper, cardboard, fabric, and plastic. Papier mâché is made from newspaper mixed with white glue and water. It's very strong when it's dry. Glue sticks are easy to use for gluing paper.

Sticky tapes. Masking tape is very useful because it does not stick permanently like other kinds of plastic tape. You can use it to hold things together while the glue dries, and then remove it easily. Clear sticky tape can also be used if you want to stick things together for good. You can get lots of brightly colored sticky tape for decorating your musical instruments. Insulating tape, which electricians use, is ideal and comes in different widths.

Scissors and craft knives. Always be very careful when you are using scissors. Use ones which have rounded ends. If you

need to use pointed scissors or a craft knife to pierce cans or cut out circles, for example, *always* ask a grown-up to do this for you.

Pencil, ruler and eraser. Always use a ruler if you need to measure anything and draw straight lines. Use a sharp pencil with a soft lead to make marks that you do not want to show and erase them later.

Apron. Always wear an apron or an old shirt over your clothes in case you make a mess. Then you will have something to wipe your hands on!

Cloth. It is always a good idea to have a cloth handy when you are using paints and glues, just in case you have an accident and need to clean it up quickly.

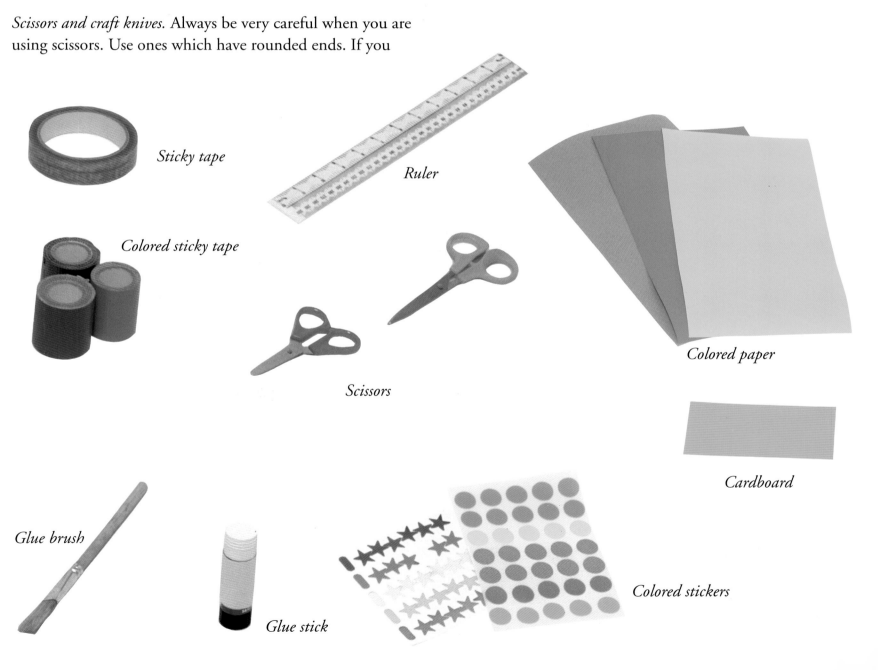

Sticky tape

Ruler

Colored sticky tape

Scissors

Colored paper

Cardboard

Glue brush

Glue stick

Colored stickers

Materials from Around the Home

All the musical instruments in this book are made using materials and equipment you will find at home. Ordinary objects like saucepan lids, cardboard boxes and soda cans make wonderful sounds if you know what to do with them. Look out for packaging and containers which you can use for making music. Cardboard tubes are really useful – collect long ones from wrapping paper, medium-sized ones from paper towels or foil, and small ones from toilet-tissue rolls. Ask a grown-up for spare bits of knitting wool, ribbon, cord and beads from the sewing box, and garden hose pipe and flowerpots from the garden shed.

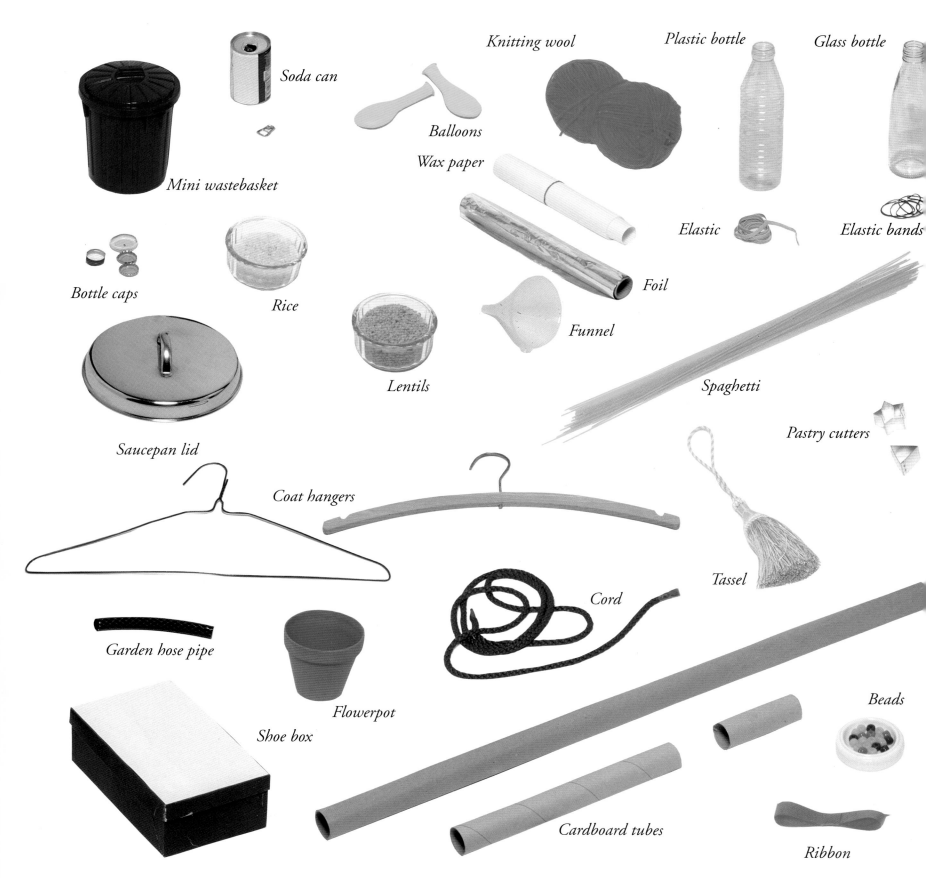

Soda can

Knitting wool

Plastic bottle

Glass bottle

Balloons

Wax paper

Mini wastebasket

Elastic

Elastic bands

Bottle caps

Rice

Foil

Funnel

Lentils

Spaghetti

Pastry cutters

Saucepan lid

Coat hangers

Tassel

Cord

Garden hose pipe

Flowerpot

Beads

Shoe box

Cardboard tubes

Ribbon

Cutting Out a Circle

It is difficult to cut a circle out of thick cardboard. The best way to do it is to ask a grown-up to punch a small hole in the center of the circle, using the point of a sharp pair of scissors. Make several small cuts outward toward the edge of the circle. You will now be able to cut around the edge of the circle quite easily.

Cut out toward the edge of the circle.

Then carefully cut around the circle itself.

Painting Straight Lines

Masking tape is very useful for this. Stick the tape along the line, then paint right up to it. You can paint a little over the edge. Wait for the paint to dry completely, then pull off the tape, and you will have a perfectly straight line. This is a good way to paint shapes like triangles and diamonds.

Use masking tape to help paint straight lines.

Painting Plastic

To make paint stick to plastic surfaces, add the same amount of white glue as the amount of paint, and stir well. If the mixture is too thick, add a little water.

Varnishing

White glue can also be used to make varnish which will protect the surface of your musical instruments. Mix the glue with twice the amount of water. The varnish will look white when you paint it on, but when it dries it will be clear.

Mix white glue with water to make a varnish.

Using Tape

Using sticky tape can be tricky, and it's quite easy to get it all tangled up! Here are some ideas to help you.

If you are covering something in tape, do not cut it first. Wait until you have finished, and then cut it.

If you only need a small piece of tape, make a small cut with the scissors. Now grip the tape firmly with both hands, and tear a piece off.

A Note for Grown-ups

Most of the musical instruments in this book can be made by a child alone with a little bit of adult help. However, always supervise your children closely whenever they are using craft materials. The places in the book where your assistance is vital, such as when sharp scissors or a craft knife are needed, are marked !.

Clashing Castanets

Castanets come from Spain, where they are used in flamenco dancing. The dancers stamp their feet and click their castanets in time to the music. It's very exciting to watch them. See if you can dance the same way. Izabella has made her castanets with metal pastry cutters so they make a wonderful sound. *Olé*!

YOU WILL NEED THESE MATERIALS AND TOOLS

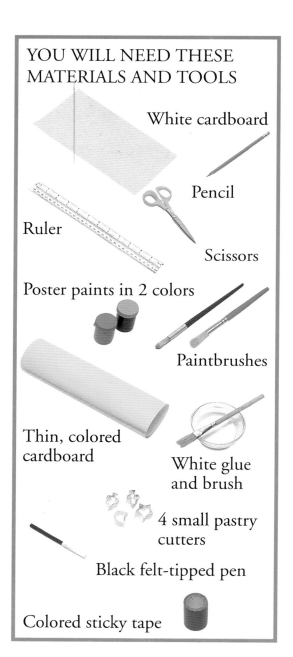

White cardboard

Pencil

Ruler

Scissors

Poster paints in 2 colors

Paintbrushes

Thin, colored cardboard

White glue and brush

4 small pastry cutters

Black felt-tipped pen

Colored sticky tape

Making music
Clash the pastry cutters together in time to the music. You can also play them by resting your hand on a table.

! Children may need help measuring out, cutting, and scoring the cardboard.

Put your thumb and middle finger through the yellow finger holders, and play away!

1 Draw a rectangle 8 in long and 3 in wide on white cardboard. Draw two lines 1½ in apart down the center of the rectangle.

2 Carefully cut out the rectangle. Bend the cardboard along the center lines. It helps if you score along the lines with the ruler first.

3 Paint one side of the cardboard. Allow to dry. Then paint the other side in a different color. Allow to dry while you make the finger holders.

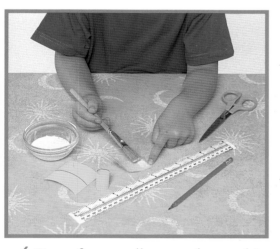

4 Draw four small rectangles on thin cardboard and cut out. Fold around into tubes to fit your middle finger and thumb. Glue together.

5 Decorate one side of the painted cardboard. Draw around the pastry cutters with a black felt-tipped pen to make outline shapes.

6 Reinforce the center where the castanets bend with colored sticky tape. This will make them last longer.

7 Glue the finger holders on to the decorated side of the cardboard. Place them about ½ in on each side of the bend. Allow to dry.

8 Glue a pastry cutter to the inside ends of each castanet. Use plenty of glue, and let it dry properly.

Wastebasket Drum

Drums are very old instruments. They are used for the rhythm in dance music, and they help soldiers to keep in step when they march. Drums were also once used to send signals because you can hear them far away. You can, like Jessica and Alice, play your drum with bare hands or with beaters.

Making music

Do not hit the drum too hard. You will get the best sound if you hit it close to the edge. If you hit different parts of the drum skin, you will get different sounds. Try playing it with a pair of chopsticks or your hands.

> ! A grown-up should cut the cork in half with a craft knife, and push the skewers into the corks to make the beaters. Children may need help with the scissors.

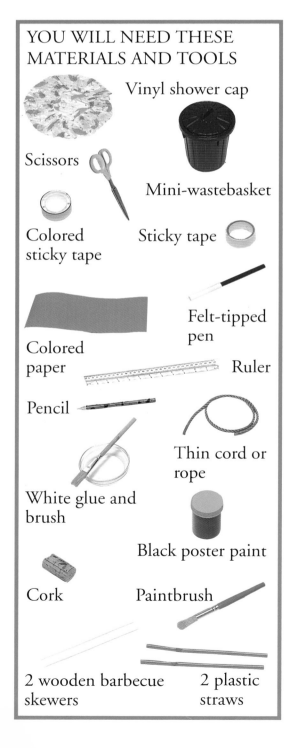

YOU WILL NEED THESE MATERIALS AND TOOLS

Vinyl shower cap

Scissors

Mini-wastebasket

Colored sticky tape

Sticky tape

Colored paper

Felt-tipped pen

Ruler

Pencil

Thin cord or rope

White glue and brush

Black poster paint

Cork

Paintbrush

2 wooden barbecue skewers

2 plastic straws

The finished drum looks very smart.

1 Cut the elastic out of the shower cap. Draw around a plate which is 2 in bigger than the top of the wastebasket. Cut the circle out.

2 Decorate the wastebasket with strips of colored sticky tape.

3 Stretch the plastic circle tightly over the open end of the wastebasket. Stick in place with pieces of sticky tape.

4 Make sure the plastic drum skin is really tight. Then tape right around the edge to hold it in place.

5 Cut a strip of colored paper to fit around the wastebasket top. Make cuts on both sides for a fringe.

6 Glue the fringe around the top of the wastebasket.

7 Tie the cord or rope around the center of the fringe.

8 Ask a grown-up to cut the cork in half across the middle. Paint the corks black. Push the skewers through the straws. Then ask a grown-up to push them into the corks.

Guiro Scraper

In Latin America, guiros are often made out of dried gourds with notches cut in the side. Gourds are a type of large fruit with a hard shell. The musicians scrape the notches with a stick to make a harsh noise. Sometimes the sound is like the call of a woodpecker or jungle bird. Alice has painted her tube in bright colors like a real guiro player.

Guiros are used to provide rhythm in Latin-American dance music.

Making music

Scrape the stick backward and forward across the slit. The string will vibrate and make a noise. A guiro made from a hard material, like thick bamboo, will make a louder sound. Ask a grown-up to cut a long slit along the bamboo pole to help the vibrating air escape and some small notches across the pole.

⚠ Children will need help cutting the slit in the cardboard tube.

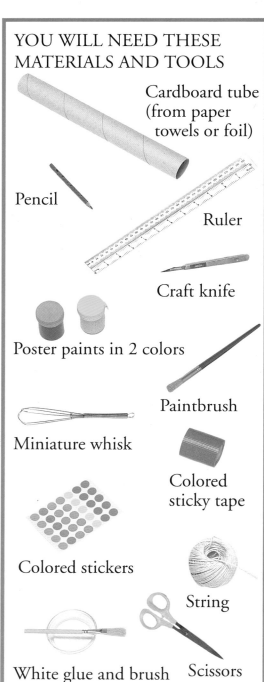

YOU WILL NEED THESE
MATERIALS AND TOOLS

Cardboard tube (from paper towels or foil)

Pencil

Ruler

Craft knife

Poster paints in 2 colors

Paintbrush

Miniature whisk

Colored sticky tape

Colored stickers

String

White glue and brush

Scissors

1 Draw a line about 8 in down the side of the cardboard tube. Ask a grown-up to cut a slit along the line with a craft knife.

2 Paint the whole tube in one color. Put it on one side to dry while you make the rhythm stick.

3 Decorate the end of the whisk with colored sticky tape. Wind it around several times. This will make it comfortable to hold.

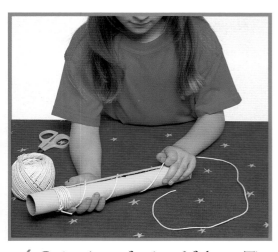

4 Cut a piece of string 6 ft long. Tie it tightly to the tube 2 in above the slit. Wind the string around the tube up to the slit. Then wind it diagonally across the slit.

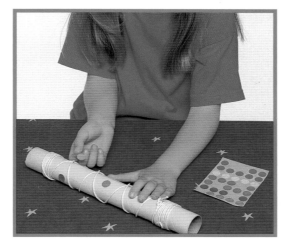

5 Wind the string around the other end of the tube. Then wind it diagonally back across the slit to make a crisscross pattern. Fasten tightly with a knot. Decorate between the string with colored stickers.

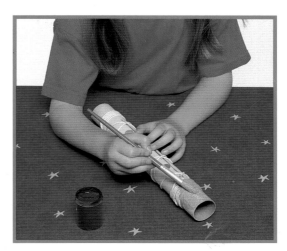

6 Paint the ends of the tube a different color. Mix the paint with the same amount of glue and a little water to make it stick.

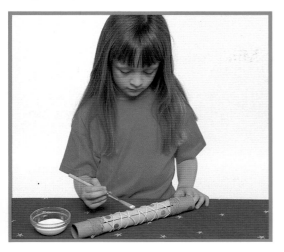

7 Paint the rest of the tube with glue. The glue will hold the string and the stickers in place.

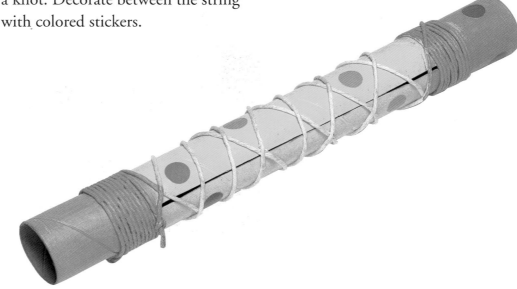

Deep Box Bass

Bass instruments play the very lowest notes. This is because they are so large. The large box and the large hole mean there is plenty of space for the air to vibrate and make a deep, booming sound. Nicholas is plucking his box bass with his fingers, like a double-bass player in a jazz band.

Your box bass is all ready for a jazz session!

Making music

Hold the elastic with one hand, and twang it with the other. You can change the sound by pressing the elastic in different places. Thick elastic makes a lower sound than thin elastic.

! A grown-up should cut the cork in half with a craft knife. Children may need help with the scissors.

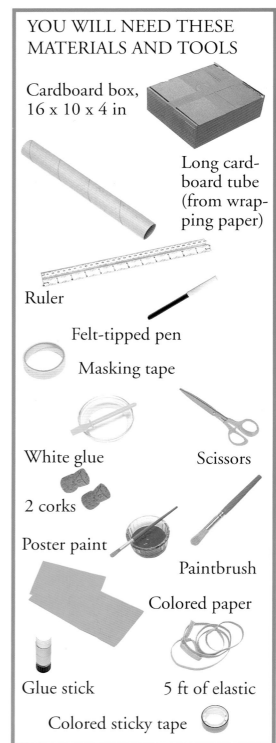

YOU WILL NEED THESE MATERIALS AND TOOLS

Cardboard box, 16 x 10 x 4 in

Long cardboard tube (from wrapping paper)

Ruler

Felt-tipped pen

Masking tape

White glue

Scissors

2 corks

Poster paint

Paintbrush

Colored paper

Glue stick

5 ft of elastic

Colored sticky tape

1 Draw around the cardboard tube to make a circle on the center of the box top. Then draw around the roll of masking tape to make a larger circle on the box front. Position it as shown.

2 Carefully cut out both circles. Pierce the circle with the scissors, and make small cuts out toward the edge of the circle. Then cut around the edge of the circle.

3 Push the tube through the small hole. Glue and tape the tube in place. Ask a grown-up to cut a cork in half. Glue and tape one half, as shown, and the other below the large hole.

4 Paint the box and the tube, and allow to dry.

5 Draw musical notes on the colored paper. Draw around a cork to make the circle shapes.

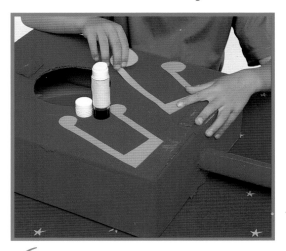

6 Cut out the notes, and glue them on to the front of the box.

7 Ask a grown-up to cut a 3 in slit down the front of the tube. Tie the elastic around the bottom of the tube. Tie a double knot in the other

8 Decorate the box with tape. Stretch the elastic down the back of the box and back up the front. Slip the knot into the slit in the tube.

17

Singing Kazoo

This is a very unusual instrument. You sing through it, and it makes your voice sound very strange. Indian musicians play a kind of kazoo which they hold against their throats when they sing. Lorenzo has covered his kazoo with stencils. This is a very easy and quick way to decorate things.

Making music
Sing through the hole in the middle of the kazoo. You can play any tune you like. Experiment with a smaller tube from a toilet-tissue roll, and see if it sounds different.

! A grown-up should make the hole in the cardboard tube and sticky tape. Children may need help with the scissors.

YOU WILL NEED THESE MATERIALS AND TOOLS

Cardboard tube (from paper towels or foil)

Scissors

Paintbrushes

Poster paints, in white and 2 colors

Paper doily

Masking tape

Waxed paper

Felt-tipped pen

White glue and brush

16 in of paper ribbon

Colored sticky tape

Stencils are a good way to decorate any of the instruments.

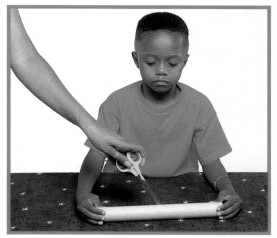

1 Ask a grown-up to make a small hole in the center of the cardboard tube.

2 Use the end of a paintbrush to smooth the edges of the hole.

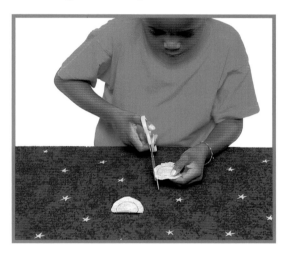

3 Paint the cardboard tube. Allow the paint to dry.

4 Cut flower shapes from the paper doily to use as stencils. Stick them on to the tube with masking tape, and paint over them. Allow the paint to dry. Then remove the stencils.

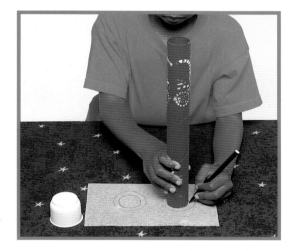

5 Draw two circles on the waxed paper. Draw around a cup or any round object that is slightly larger than the end of the tube. Now draw around the end of the tube to make a smaller circle inside each larger one.

6 Cut out the large circles. Make small cuts between the large and small circles. This will give each circle a frill around the edge. Brush glue on to the frills.

7 Stretch the waxed-paper circles tightly across the ends of the cardboard tube. Press the frills around the sides of the tube.

8 Glue ribbon around the ends of the tube. Stick a piece of colored sticky tape over the hole. Ask a grown-up to pierce through the tape.

19

Twirling Japanese Drum

Different parts of the world have different kinds of music and different instruments. Lorenzo's little Japanese drum has a handle so that he can twirl it between his fingers. It makes a great rattling sound. When the drum is moving fast, the paper swirls look as if they are spinning around.

You could add extra strings and more beads to your drum, if you like.

Making music
Hold the handle of the drum between your palms, and twirl it backward and forward. The beads will fly up and hit the drum.

! A grown-up should make the holes in the side of the box lid and base. Children may need help with scissors.

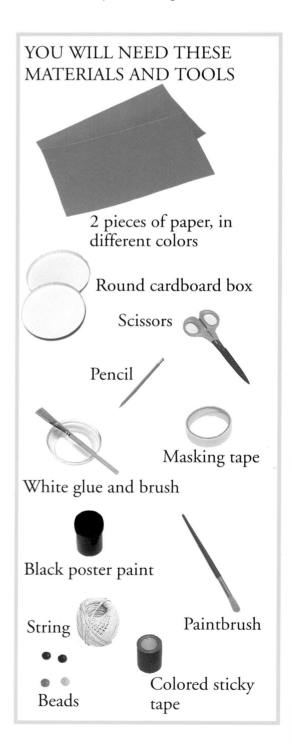

YOU WILL NEED THESE
MATERIALS AND TOOLS

2 pieces of paper, in
different colors

Round cardboard box

Scissors

Pencil

Masking tape

White glue and brush

Black poster paint

Paintbrush

String

Beads

Colored sticky
tape

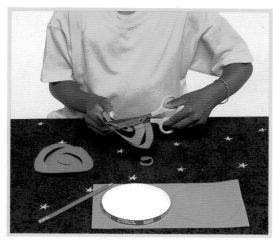

1 Draw twice around the box lid on one piece of paper. Cut out the circles. Cut them into swirls. Cut two circles from the other piece of paper.

2 Ask a grown-upp to make a hole in the side of the box lid and one in the side of the base, large enough to push the pencil through. Put on the lid.

3 Push the pencil through the holes, and secure it with glue and masking tape. Tape around the side of the box, and paint the tape black.

4 Cut a piece of string about 12 in long. Tie a double knot at one end. Thread one or two beads on to the string. Then tie another knot. Repeat at the other end of the string.

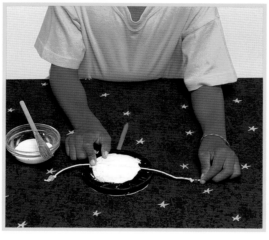

5 Spread glue over one side of the box. Lay the string carefully across the middle so that it is in the center, with the same amount of string showing on each side.

6 Cover the glue and string with one of the whole circles of colored paper. Glue one paper swirl on top. Glue a paper circle and a swirl to the other side of the box. Allow to dry.

7 Decorate the pencil handle with colored sticky tape. Leave some of the pencil showing to make stripes.

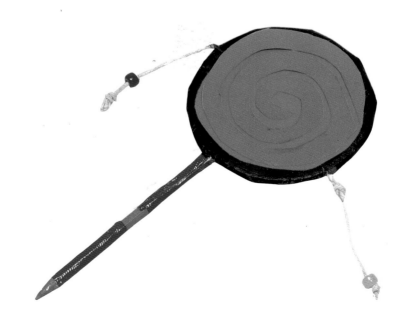

Metal Wind Chimes

You do not have to play these wind chimes yourself – if you hang them up, the wind will play them for you. The best place to hang them is from a door frame or window frame. When there is a breeze, the chimes make a tinkling sound. Benjamin likes to play his chimes himself, using a spoon.

Ask a grown-up for an old metal spoon which you can decorate with colored stickers.

Making music

Run a metal spoon along the chimes and back again, or you can strike each chime piece separately.

A grown-up should remove the ring pulls from the soda cans and cover any sharp edges with thick sticky tape. A grown-up should also pierce the bottle caps and soda cans with a corkscrew or other sharp object such as a skewer.

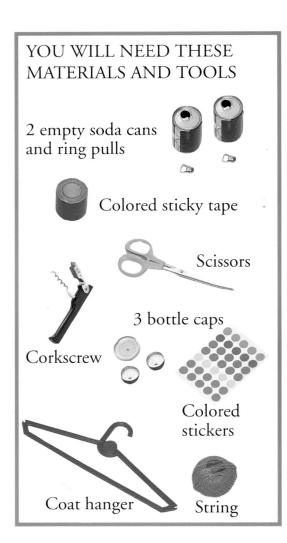

YOU WILL NEED THESE
MATERIALS AND TOOLS

2 empty soda cans
and ring pulls

Colored sticky tape

Scissors

3 bottle caps

Corkscrew

Colored stickers

Coat hanger   String

1 Wash the soda cans, and allow to dry. Cover them with colored sticky tape.

2 Ask a grown-up to make a hole in each of the bottle caps, using the corkscrew.

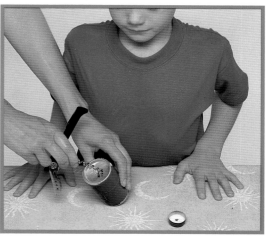

3 Ask a grown-up to make a hole in the bottoms of the soda cans, using the corkscrew.

4 Decorate the cans and the bottle caps with lots of colored stickers.

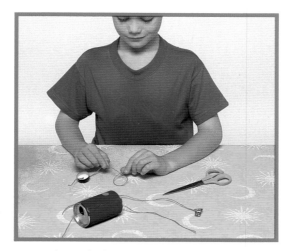

5 Thread the cans, ring pulls and bottle caps on to pieces of string. Knot the string to keep them in place.

6 Tie all the pieces of string on to the coat hanger.

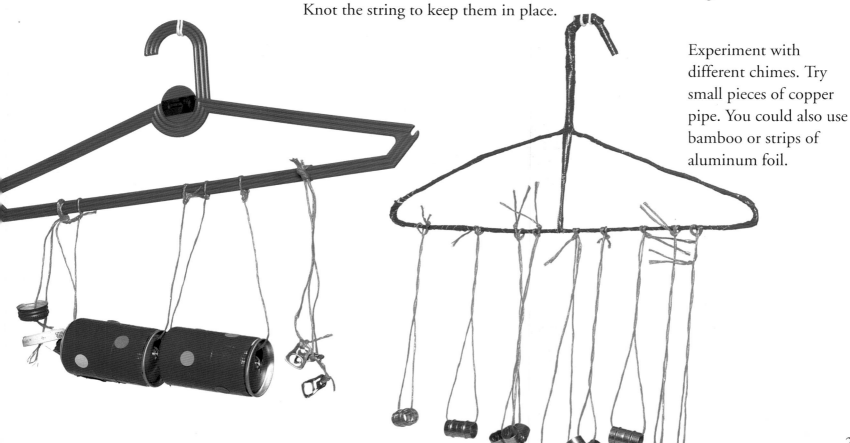

Experiment with different chimes. Try small pieces of copper pipe. You could also use bamboo or strips of aluminum foil.

Shoe-box Guitar

The guitar is probably the most popular instrument of all. It's easy to carry, and you can play many different kinds of music on it. Jessica is plucking the elastic string on her guitar, just like a pop star. Electric guitars don't have boxes full of air like this one, so they need electricity to make them sound loud.

YOU WILL NEED THESE MATERIALS AND TOOLS

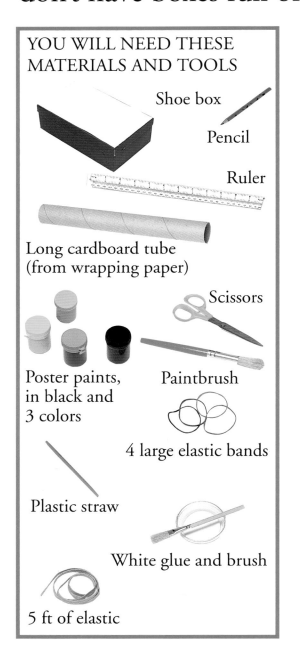

Shoe box

Pencil

Ruler

Long cardboard tube (from wrapping paper)

Scissors

Poster paints, in black and 3 colors

Paintbrush

4 large elastic bands

Plastic straw

White glue and brush

5 ft of elastic

Making music

Pluck the elastic string with one hand. With your other hand, press the elastic against the cardboard tube. If you press in different places, you can change the note. Try strumming the string with a coin instead of plucking it.

! Children may need help cutting out the circles. See the "Introduction" for an easy way of doing this.

A guitar is a large box full of air. The air vibrates and makes the sound which escapes through the hole.

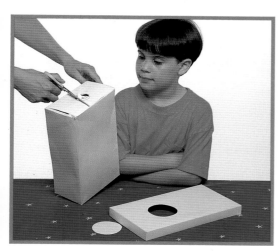

1 Draw a 4 in circle on the box lid. Draw around the tube on one end of the base of the box. Ask a grown-up to cut out the circles.

2 Draw a guitar shape on the lid of the box. Use a circular shape as a guide, or use a pair of compasses, if you like.

3 Outline the guitar shape in black paint. Fill in with colored paint. Then paint the rest of the box another color. Paint the tube.

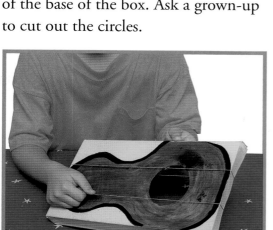

4 Stretch two elastic bands across the lid. Position them as shown, just on the edges of the hole.

5 Put the lid on the box. Hold it in place with two more elastic bands. Cut the straw in half. Slide the two pieces under the elastic bands at each end of the guitar. Glue in place.

6 Cut a slit about 3 in long at one end of the tube. Tie a knot in one end of the elastic. Make a loop in the other end, and slide it over the end of the tube.

7 Push the tube into the hole in the box. Stretch the elastic around the back of the box and up around the front. Slip the knot into the slit in the tube.

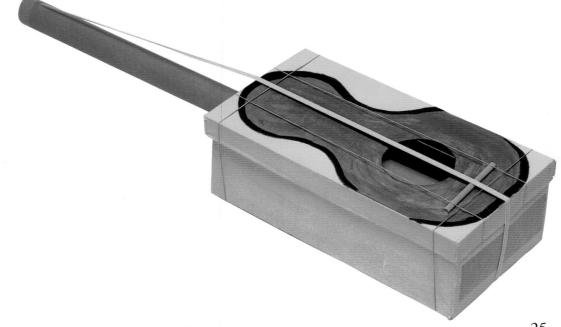

Caxixi Rattle

The name of this rattle is pronounced "casheeshee." It comes from Latin America. You can fill it with anything that will make a good sound – try rice, beans, or sand. Alice has made a face for her rattle with scraps of paper and stickers. She has also given it a wonderful fringe.

⚠ A grown-up should puncture the bottle, and children may need help with the scissors.

Shake your caxixi rattle in time to your favorite music.

Making music

Make two caxixi rattles, and shake them together. Practice until you can keep in time to the rhythm of the music. Fill the bottles with different things to make different sounds.

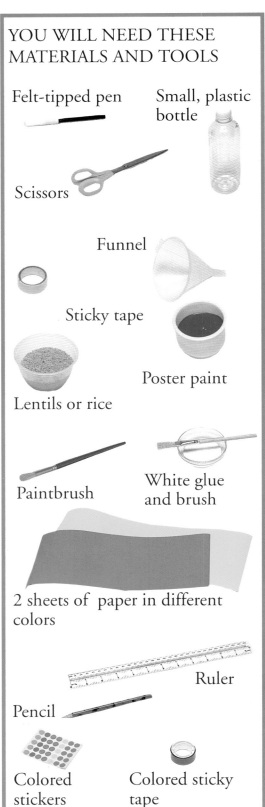

YOU WILL NEED THESE MATERIALS AND TOOLS

Felt-tipped pen

Small, plastic bottle

Scissors

Funnel

Sticky tape

Poster paint

Lentils or rice

Paintbrush

White glue and brush

2 sheets of paper in different colors

Ruler

Pencil

Colored stickers

Colored sticky tape

1 Wash and dry the bottle. Draw a line around the bottle about one third from the top. Draw another line the same distance from the bottom.

2 Ask a grown-up to puncture the bottle with the point of the scissors. Then cut along both the lines you have marked.

3 Stick the top and bottom pieces of the bottle together with sticky tape to make a shorter bottle shape. Pour the lentils or rice into the bottle.

4 Mix the paint with glue and a little water and paint the top half of the bottle. Allow to dry.

5 Cut a strip of each of the colored sheets of paper, long enough to wrap around the bottle.

6 To make a fringe, fold the strips over and make plenty of small cuts halfway across the strips of paper.

7 Glue the fringe around the bottle. Hold it in place with colored tape. Decorate your caxixi with a funny face, using the colored stickers, the paper, and the felt-tipped pen.

This is a different caxixi shape made from a soda can and decorated with star stickers and colored sticky tape.

Tambourine Flower

Tambourines have been played since the Middle Ages. They were made of a circle of wood with very thin animal skin stretched across, and they had bells around the edge. Like castanets, tambourines are very popular in Spanish dancing. You could play them together. Leslie has painted his tambourine to look like a sunflower.

Instead of bottle caps, you could use beads or buttons. They will all make different sounds.

Making music

Hold your tambourine above your head, and shake it. You can also hold it in one hand and tap it with the fingers of your other hand. You can even bang it against your knee.

! A grown-up should pierce the bottle caps with a corkscrew or other sharp object. Children may need help with the scissors.

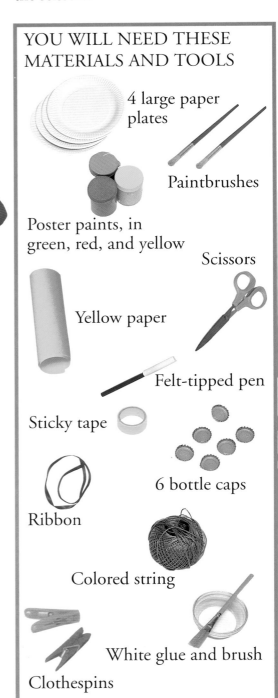

YOU WILL NEED THESE MATERIALS AND TOOLS

4 large paper plates

Paintbrushes

Poster paints, in green, red, and yellow

Scissors

Yellow paper

Felt-tipped pen

Sticky tape

6 bottle caps

Ribbon

Colored string

White glue and brush

Clothespins

1 Using green paint, paint around the rim of one of the paper plates. Do not paint the middle. Allow the paint to dry.

2 Cut a long strip of yellow paper. Fold the strip over and over. Draw a petal shape on the top layer, and cut out through all the layers. Repeat to make sixteen petals.

3 Tape the petal shapes around the unpainted circle in the middle of the plate.

4 Take another paper plate. Cut out the center circle, and paint it red. Allow to dry.

5 Paint spots of yellow on the red circle. Paint the bottle caps red, as well. Allow to dry.

6 Cut the ribbon into several pieces, each roughly the same length. Cut two pieces of string the same length, and knot at one end. Ask a grown-up to pierce the bottle caps. Thread three on to each piece of string, tying a knot after each one.

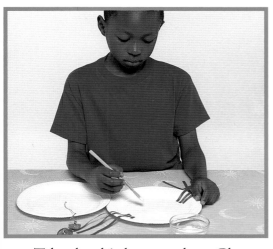

7 Take the third paper plate. Glue three or four ribbons on each side. Glue the string on each side of the fourth plate. Glue the plates together.

8 Put clothespins around the edge to make sure the plates stick together properly. Allow the glue to dry.

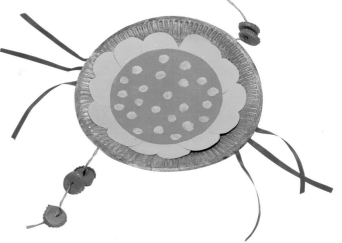

Saucepan-lid Cymbals

Saucepan lids make terrific cymbals. You can hit one with a beater, or clash them together as Benjamin is doing. Be careful not to bang them directly together. To do a proper cymbal clash, you move one cymbal up and one down. Real cymbals can turn inside out if you hit them directly together! Cymbals are often played with drums in a drum kit.

YOU WILL NEED THESE MATERIALS AND TOOLS

2 matching metal saucepan lids

Ribbon

Colored stickers

Scissors

Narrow and wide colored sticky tape

Large bottle washer

Wooden barbecue skewer

Scouring pad

Cork

Making music

Cymbals are often played very loudly, but they can also make a lovely, soft sound. You can also hold a cymbal by its handle, or hang it from a piece of string, and strike it with one of your homemade beaters.

! A grown-up should cut the cork in half using a craft knife. Children will also need help pushing the skewer into the cork.

If you want to decorate your saucepan lid cymbals, check with a grown-up first to make sure they don't mind!

1 Decorate the saucepan lids with colored stickers. Arrange them in a circle, following the shape of the lid. Decorate the ribbon with stickers.

2 Decorate the handles with strips of ribbon, looping them around the handle. Stick them together with narrow colored sticky tape.

3 Cover the rest of the handles with wide colored sticky tape. Wind the narrow tape around the handle to make stripes, if you like.

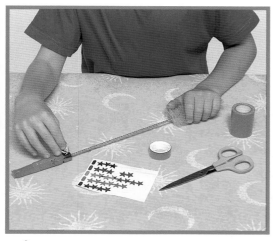

4 Now make the first stick. Decorate the handle of the bottle washer with colored stickers and sticky tape.

5 Make the second stick. Push the wooden skewer through the middle of the scouring pad. Ask a grown-up to cut the cork in half. Push the sharp end of the skewer into one piece of cork.

6 Wind colored sticky tape around the cork and the skewer where it comes out below the scouring pad. This will stop the scouring pad from slipping down the handle.

The two beaters make different sounds.

Snakey Maracas

Maracas are played by shaking them in time to music. The rice inside them rattles around to make the sound. Maracas are very popular in Africa and Latin America, where they are often made out of gourds. Nicholas has made his maracas out of papier mâché. This is wet newspaper mixed with glue. When it is dry, it sets hard so that you can paint it.

! Children may need help blowing up and tying the balloons and with cutting the holes in the papier mâché.

When you play your maracas, the snakes will wriggle about and frighten your audience.

Making music
Shake both maracas together in time to the music. You can also play one maraca on its own. Hold it in one hand, and roll it against the palm of your other hand.

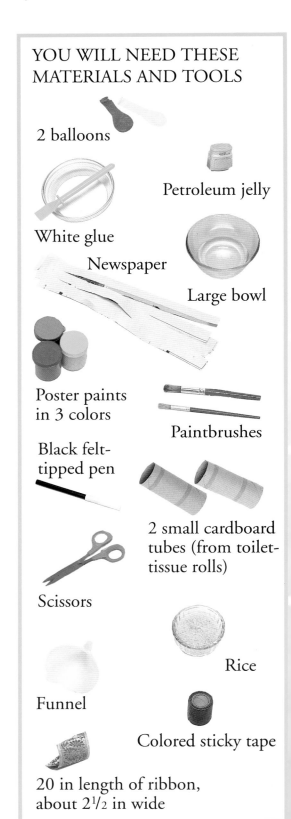

YOU WILL NEED THESE
MATERIALS AND TOOLS

2 balloons

Petroleum jelly

White glue

Newspaper

Large bowl

Poster paints
in 3 colors

Paintbrushes

Black felt-
tipped pen

2 small cardboard
tubes (from toilet-
tissue rolls)

Scissors

Rice

Funnel

Colored sticky tape

20 in length of ribbon,
about 2½ in wide

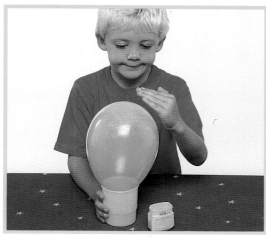

1 Blow up and tie the balloons. Cover them with petroleum jelly. Support the balloons in jars or mugs, otherwise they will bounce about.

2 Tear the newspaper into strips and squares. Soak them in glue. Cover the balloons with strips. Allow to dry. Then cover them with squares.

3 Wait for the second layer to dry. Then paint the balloons. Allow the paint to dry.

4 Now paint the cardboard tubes, using a different color. Allow the paint to dry.

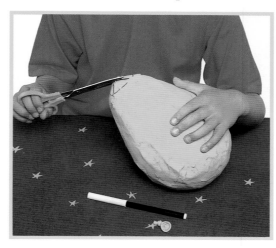

5 Draw around one of the cardboard tubes on the end of each balloon, and cut out the circles.

6 Spread glue on to one end of each cardboard tube. Push them into the holes in the balloons for handles.

7 Pour the rice into the balloons through the handles. Seal the end of each handle with colored sticky tape. Spread glue on to the handles, then cover them with ribbon.

8 Paint squiggly snakes to decorate the maracas. Use the black felt-tipped pen to draw the snakes' eyes and their forked tongues.

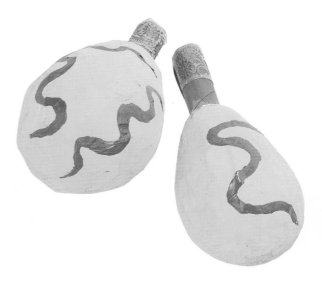

Bottle Xylophone

Bottles make wonderful musical instruments. To get different notes, you add more water. Play the xylophone with different sticks to make different sounds. You can also blow across the top of the bottles.

Gabriella has put colored water in her xylophone bottles. This looks pretty, and it also helps her remember the different notes.

! A grown-up should push the skewer into the cork. Never leave the colored water in the bottles in case someone is tempted to try a taste. The water is *not* drinkable.

The different sticks make different sounds. What other sticks could you use?

Making music

See if you can play a simple tune like "Three Blind Mice." Add a little water to each bottle or pour some out until you get the notes right.

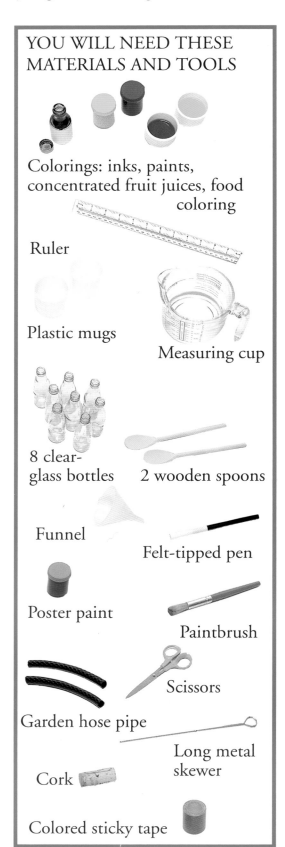

YOU WILL NEED THESE MATERIALS AND TOOLS

Colorings: inks, paints, concentrated fruit juices, food coloring

Ruler

Plastic mugs

Measuring cup

8 clear-glass bottles

2 wooden spoons

Funnel

Felt-tipped pen

Poster paint

Paintbrush

Scissors

Garden hose pipe

Cork

Long metal skewer

Colored sticky tape

1 Mix seven different colors with water. Use inks, paints, concentrated fruit juices or food coloring.

2 Hit one of the glass bottles with a wooden spoon, and listen to the sound it makes.

3 Mark a line ³/4 in from the bottom of the bottle. Use a felt-tipped pen.

4 Pour water into the bottle up to the mark. This is much easier if you use a funnel. Hit the bottle again. This time, the sound will be lower.

5 Pour a different-colored water into each bottle. Raise the level of the water by ³/4 in each time. The bottle with the most water will give the lowest note.

6 Now try blowing across the top of each bottle. This time, the bottle with the most water will give the highest note!

7 Paint the round ends of two wooden spoons. Cover the handles with hose pipe.

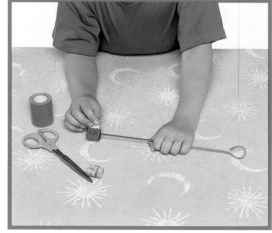

8 Make a different stick. Ask a grown-up to cut the cork in half and push in the skewer. Cover the cork with sticky tape.

Reed Pipe Man

Some instruments have a reed to help make the sound. A straw makes a good reed, but instead of sucking on it, remember to blow through it! This pipe is a very simple kind of oboe, and it makes quite a loud noise. Joshua has drawn a face on his pipe and given it a smart, frilly collar.

Making music

Put the end of the straw in your mouth, and grip it between your lips. Take a deep breath and blow *slowly*. You should sound just like a duck!

[!] Children may need help with the scissors.

The reed pipe man is ready to make some music for you.

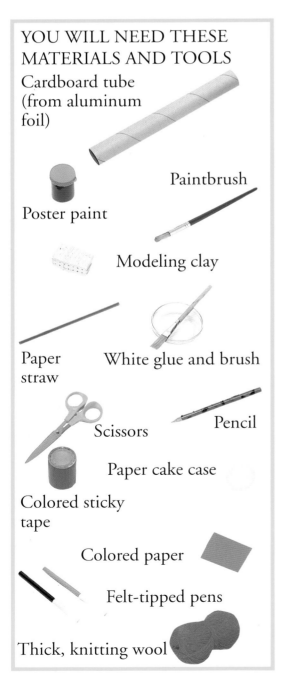

YOU WILL NEED THESE MATERIALS AND TOOLS

Cardboard tube (from aluminum foil)

Poster paint

Paintbrush

Modeling clay

Paper straw

White glue and brush

Scissors

Pencil

Paper cake case

Colored sticky tape

Colored paper

Felt-tipped pens

Thick, knitting wool

1 Paint the cardboard tube. Allow the paint to dry.

2 Press out a thick layer of modeling clay. Push the end of the tube into the modeling clay, and cut out a circle.

3 Glue the modeling-clay circle into one end of the tube. Allow the glue to dry.

4 Cut the straw in half. Squash the end of one piece flat under a big book. Then snip off the corners of the flattened end. This will be the reed.

5 Make a hole in the center of the modeling clay with the pencil. Push the straw through the hole, and pinch the modeling clay around it.

6 Cut out the center of the paper cake case. The frilly edge will make a good collar.

7 Cut the colored sticky tape and colored paper into diamond shapes, and use them to decorate the tube. Tape the paper collar around the tube about a third of the way down.

8 Draw a face on the tube, above the collar. Cut short pieces of wool, and glue them on for the hair.

Bugle Blow

The first bugles were used to send signals in battle or out hunting. Today, bugles are used in the army to wake everyone up in the morning! The soldier's bugle is a brass instrument but Claudius's bugle is made from garden hose pipe. To get a good sound from this kind of instrument, you need a mouthpiece.

You will need plenty of puff to play your bugle.

Making music

Rest the rim of the mouthpiece on your lips, and take a deep breath. Buzz your lips into the mouthpiece. To play higher notes, blow faster.

Children may need help cutting and positioning the hose pipe.

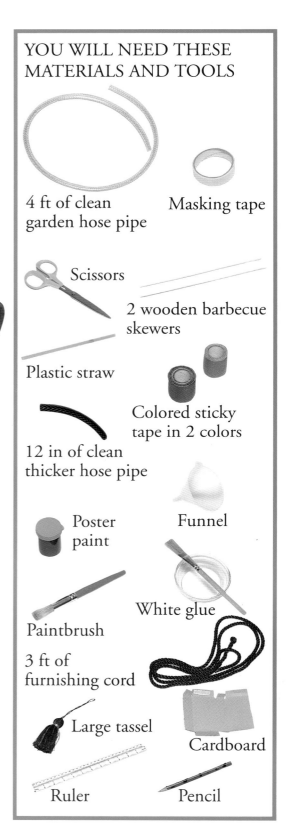

YOU WILL NEED THESE
MATERIALS AND TOOLS

4 ft of clean
garden hose pipe

Masking tape

Scissors

2 wooden barbecue
skewers

Plastic straw

Colored sticky
tape in 2 colors

12 in of clean
thicker hose pipe

Poster
paint

Funnel

White glue

Paintbrush

3 ft of
furnishing cord

Large tassel

Cardboard

Ruler

Pencil

1 Bend the thin hose pipe into a circle so that the ends overlap, as shown. Bind the circle together with two pieces of masking tape 3 in apart.

2 Push both skewers into the straw. Place the straw behind the joint in the hose pipe, and tape them together in three places.

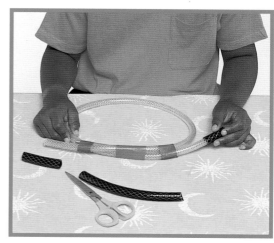

3 Cut a piece of thick hose pipe about 6 in long. Slide it on to one end of the hose pipe. Cut a shorter length, and slide it on to the other end.

4 Mix the poster paint with the same amount of glue and a little water.. Then paint the funnel. Push the funnel into the longer piece of thick hose pipe.

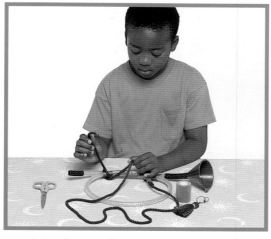

5 Tie the cord on to the bugle so that you can carry it across your chest. Fasten the tassel to the bugle.

6 Measure a square about 5 x 5 in on the cardboard and cut out.

7 Roll the square into a cone shape. Trim off any extra cardboard. Tape the cone together.

8 Fit the cone into the mouthpiece end of the bugle.

Flowerpot Chimes

These flowerpot chimes are like the Metal Wind Chimes. Ilaira likes to play her chimes herself, but you can also leave them to knock together gently in the wind. The flowerpots are very heavy, so you need a strong coat hanger. If you make both sets of chimes, you can compare them. They sound very different.

Making music

Hit the flowerpots gently with the spoons. Does the small flowerpot sound different from the large one?

> **!** A grown-up should make the holes in the corks and cut them in half with a craft knife. Children may need help with the scissors.

The finished flowerpot chimes ready to play a tune. Ilaira has painted her spoons bright green.

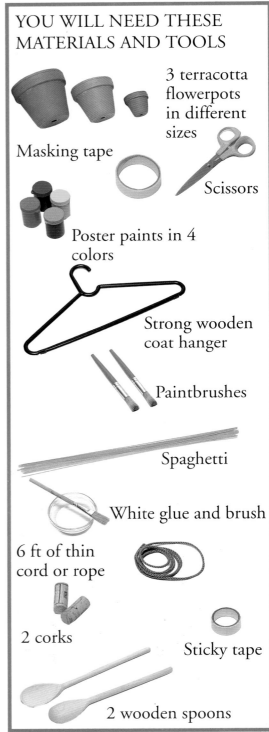

YOU WILL NEED THESE MATERIALS AND TOOLS

3 terracotta flowerpots in different sizes

Masking tape

Scissors

Poster paints in 4 colors

Strong wooden coat hanger

Paintbrushes

Spaghetti

White glue and brush

6 ft of thin cord or rope

2 corks

Sticky tape

2 wooden spoons

1 Use the masking tape to make four triangle shapes on each pot. Paint above the tape in different colors. Allow to dry. Then pull off the tape.

2 Tape along the edge of the painted area. Then paint below the tape in another color. Allow to dry, and remove the tape.

3 Decorate the coat hanger. Use as many colors as possible to make it really bright. Paint the wooden spoons too, if you like.

4 Ask a grown-up to cook some spaghetti. Keep it soft in warm water until you glue it on to the pots. Hold the spaghetti in place with masking tape until the glue dries.

5 Mix the paints together to make brown, and paint the spaghetti. Try not to paint the pots underneath. Allow to dry.

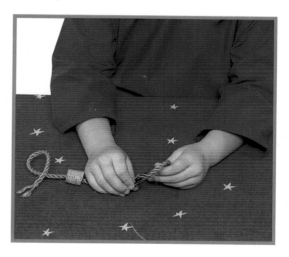

6 Cut the cord into three pieces. Ask a grown-up to make a hole in the corks and cut them in half. Thread a cork on each cord, and tie a knot in one end.

7 Thread the other end of the cord through the hole in the bottom of the flowerpot.

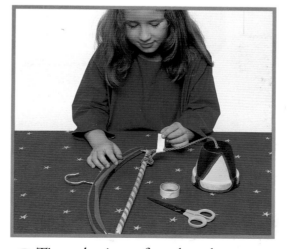

8 Tie each piece of cord to the coat hanger. Tie a good knot. Then bind the cord with sticky tape.

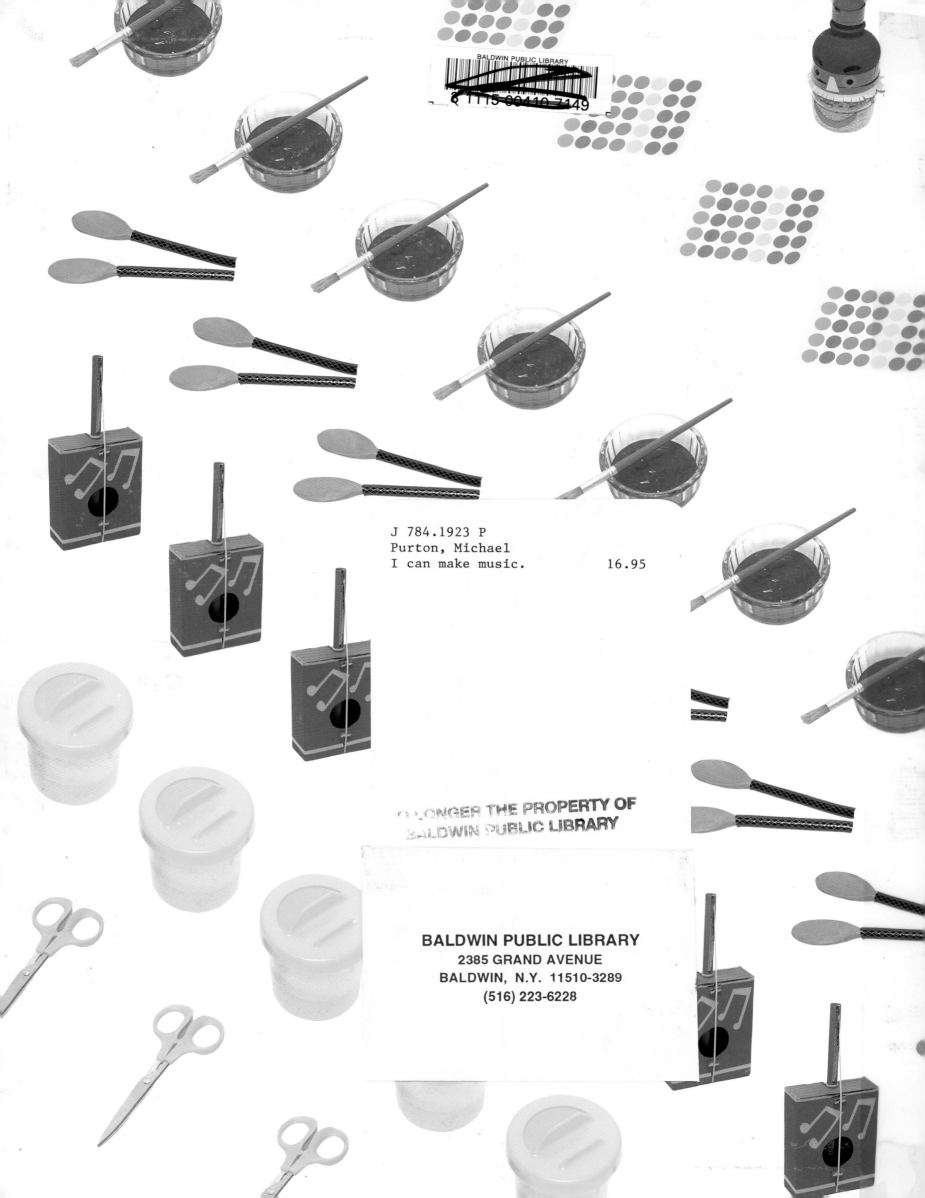